EVERY DAY two children die on the roads.
EVERY WEEK a thousand children are injured.

*Children must be taught first of all about safe
places to play. Under the age of seven, they
cannot judge the distance and speed at which
traffic travels. Encourage them to STOP, LOOK
ALL ROUND and LISTEN every time they cross
the road.*

*Even a child of seven who has learnt the Green
Cross Code should not be allowed to cross the
road alone until you have checked to make sure
he understands the Code properly and follows
it correctly. He should not cross alone even at
pedestrian crossings until you are sure of this.*

*Supporting books, wall posters and also the
armbands mentioned on pages 32 and 33 are
available from The Royal Society for the
Prevention of Accidents, Cannon House, The
Priory Queensway, Birmingham, B4 6BS, which
has approved this book. The Society will also
supply details of the National Cycling Proficiency
Scheme for children who are learning to ride
bicycles.*

Acknowledgment:

The extracts from the *Green Cross Code* are reproduced by
permission of the Controller of Her Majesty's Stationery Office.

ROAD SENSE

by R Collingridge A M Inst R S
illustrated by B H Robinson

RoSPA
APPROVED

Ladybird Books
Loughborough

I am going
to show you how
to be safe on the roads.

Roads are dangerous.
There are fast cars,
heavy lorries
and noisy motorbikes.

The Green Cross code X and

1. First find a safe place to cross, then stop. It is safer to cross at some places than others. Subways. Footbridges. Zebra and Pelican crossings. Traffic lights. Where there is a policeman, or a lollipop man, or a traffic warden. If you can't find any good crossing places like these, choose a place where you can see clearly along the roads in all directions.
Don't try to cross between parked cars. Move to a clear space and always give drivers a chance to see you clearly.

FIND A SAFE PLACE AWAY FROM PARKED CARS.

NOT HERE BRUCE!

2. Stand on the pavement near the kerb.

STOP AND WAIT NEAR THE KERB.

4. If traffic is coming, let it pass. Look all round again. If there's any traffic near, let it go past. Then look round again and listen to make sure no other traffic is coming.

AND LET TRAFFIC PASS...

5. When there is no traffic near, walk straight across the road. When there is no traffic near it's safe to cross. If there is something in the distance do not cross unless you're **certain** there's plenty of time. Remember, even if traffic is a long way off, it may be coming very fast. When it's safe, walk straight across the road – don't run.

6

w to use it.

't stand too near the edge of
pavement. Stop a little way back
n the kerb – where you'll be
ay from traffic but where you
still see if anything is coming.

STAY-
BRUCE!

3. Look all round
for traffic and
listen. Traffic
may be coming
from all
directions, so
take care to look along
every road. And
listen too, because
you can sometimes
hear traffic before
you can see it.

LOOK ALL
ROUND AND
LISTEN.

NO TRAFFIC NEAR,
WALK **STRAIGHT**
ACROSS.

6. Keep looking and
listening for
traffic while you
cross. Once you're
in the road, keep
looking and
listening in case you
didn't see some traffic – or
in case other traffic
suddenly appears.

KEEP LOOKING
AND LISTENING.

Learn the Green Cross Code
and use it every time.

Whenever you cross the road
use the Green Cross Code.

Make sure
that everyone crossing with you
uses it too.

Find a safe place to cross

Here is a Subway.
It is safe because it goes
under the road.

This footbridge takes us
over the road.
We can look down
on all the traffic.

We never throw anything
because it could cause a crash.

Zebra Crossings
must be used properly.
Wait near the kerb
until all traffic has stopped.

Never cross on the zigzags.

Use the shortest route.

Go *straight* across the road,
not at an angle.

Pelican Crossing

At Pelican Crossings
press the button and wait
for the green man.

Cars need time to stop.

RED

Don't cross

Press button
and wait
for green signal

GREEN

Cross carefully

FLASHING GREEN

*Don't start
to cross*

The lights are
about to change
to red

Cross only when you are sure
that all cars and lorries
have stopped.

Never start to cross
when the green man is flashing.

These children have crossed
to a traffic island
in the middle of the road.

They are safe here
until the rest of the road
is clear.

Never try to cross
between parked cars.

Drivers cannot see you
and you cannot see
if any cars are coming.

18

Walk to a place
where you have a good view.
Look all around before you cross.

People who help us cross the road

Here is Mr Sharp, our Lollipop man.

They wait at the kerb
until he tells them to cross.
He is telling Anne and James
that it is safe
to walk across the busy road
to school.

Roy and Shirley
have gone to this policeman
who is directing traffic.
He will see them safely
across the road.
So will a traffic warden.

You can ask older children to help,
or grown-ups if you know them.

Look all round
and listen
for traffic.

If some
is coming,
don't cross.

Let it pass.

When
you are sure
there is
no traffic,
walk straight
across.

Keep looking and listening for any more traffic

25

Never play in the road
or street.
If you have a garden,
play there
and keep the gate shut.

If your garden is not large enough
use a park or playground
away from the busy roads.

Small children must go
with a parent or grown-up.

In the country

Look at Jenny and Tim
on this country lane.

They are walking
on the right-hand side
of the road.

They can see cars
coming towards them.

They walk
close to the hedge,
and one behind the other.
They keep listening for traffic.

See and be seen

People who are wearing
something bright
can be seen easily by drivers –
especially on gloomy days.

If you are wearing hoods
make sure that you turn your head
to look before you cross.
A hood makes it harder to hear, too.

The orange parts
show up in daylight

and at night
the grey pieces shine white
when car headlights fall on them.

Peter has
an orange duffel bag.

It is easily seen.

Mary has a satchel.

It has orange material
stitched to it.

Susan and Jane have silver stripes
on their coats.

They were sewn on so that drivers
could see the children
when they are coming home
from school in the winter.

Looking after others

Don't let your dog run on the road.
Always keep him on a lead.

Walk like this with your brothers
and sisters or younger friends,
and help them
to cross the road safely.

Look after Mummy and Daddy too.
Make sure they use the crossings.

In the car

On a long journey
play a game with me.

I spy with my little eye
something beginning with b.

Always sit in the back
and wear your safety belt
or harness.

Mummy and Daddy
should wear
seat belts too.

Using the bus

Before you get on the bus
let other people off.

Hold on tightly to the rail
and wait for the bus to stop
before you try to get off.

46

If you need to cross the road
wait for the bus to go first.

Why must you boys behave badly
on the school bus?
If the driver looks round
to tell you off
he might have an accident.

Cycling

At nine, we can be trained
to ride cycles safely
in the National Cycling
Proficiency Scheme.

My class is learning at school.
Ask your teacher
or Road Safety Officer about it.